Harry Fenn

Winter Poems By Favorite American Poets

Harry Fenn

Winter Poems By Favorite American Poets

ISBN/EAN: 9783337256913

Printed in Europe, USA, Canada, Australia, Japan

Cover: Foto ©Thomas Meinert / pixelio.de

More available books at **www.hansebooks.com**

WINTER POEMS

BY

FAVORITE AMERICAN POETS

WITH ILLUSTRATIONS

CAMBRIDGE, MASS

"These keep
Seeming and savour all the winter long."
SHAKESPEARE, *The Winter's Tale.*

In "WINTER POEMS" the Publishers offer a Holiday book having special appropriateness to the season. The first poem, "THE PAGEANT," was written expressly for this volume. The other poems combine the elements of wide popularity, seasonableness, and fitness for illustration. It is believed that the variety and beauty of the designs, and the excellence of the engraving and printing, will commend the volume to the highest favor of the public.

CONTENTS.

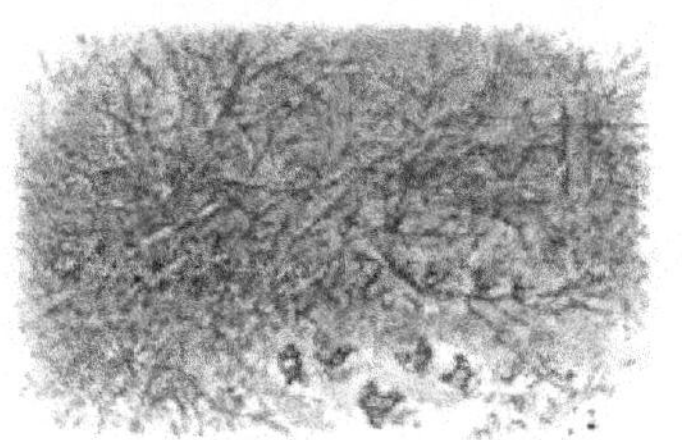

LIST OF ILLUSTRATIONS.

[The Engravings by A. V. S. ANTHONY, under whose supervision the book is prepared.]

A WINTER PIECE.

THE FIRST SNOW-FALL.

MIDNIGHT MASS FOR THE DYING YEAR.

[The Vignettes and Ornaments in the introductory pages are drawn by JOHN J. HARLEY.]

Winter Poems

THE PAGEANT.

A SOUND as if from bells of silver,
Or elfin cymbals smitten clear,
Through the frost-pictured panes I hear.

A brightness which outshines the morning,
A splendor brooking no delay,
Beckons and tempts my feet away.

I leave the trodden village highway
For virgin snow-paths glimmering through
A jewelled elm-tree avenue;

Where, keen against the walls of sapphire,
The gleaming tree-bolls, ice-embossed,
Hold up their chandeliers of frost.

I tread in Orient halls enchanted,
I dream the Saga's dream of caves
Gem-lit beneath the North Sea waves!

I walk the land of Eldorado,
    I touch its mimic garden bowers,
    Its silver leaves and diamond flowers!

The flora of the mystic mine-world
    Around me lifts on crystal stems
    The petals of its clustered gems!

What miracle of weird transforming
    Is this wild work of frost and light,
    This glimpse of glory infinite!

This foregleam of the Holy City
    Like that to him of Patmos given,
    The white bride coming down from heaven!

How flash the ranked and mail-clad alders,
    Through what sharp-glancing spears of reeds
    The brook its muffled water leads!

Yon maple, like the bush of Horeb,
    Burns unconsumed: a white, cold fire
    Rays out from every grassy spire.

Each slender rush and spike of mullein,
Low laurel shrub and drooping fern,
Transfigured, blaze where'er I turn.

How yonder Ethiopian hemlock
Crowned with his glistening circlet stands!
What jewels light his swarthy hands!

Here, where the forest opens southward,
Between its hospitable pines,
As through a door, the warm sun shines.

The jewels loosen on the branches,
And lightly, as the soft winds blow,
Fall, tinkling, on the ice below.

And through the clashing of their cymbals
I hear the old familiar fall
Of water down the rocky wall,

Where, from its wintry prison breaking,
In dark and silence hidden long,
The brook repeats its summer song.

One instant flashing in the sunshine,
Keen as a sabre from its sheath,
Then lost again the ice beneath.

I hear the rabbit lightly leaping,
The foolish screaming of the jay,
The chopper's axe-stroke far away;

The clamor of some neighboring barn-yard,
The lazy cock's belated crow,
Or cattle-tramp in crispy snow.

And, as in some enchanted forest
    The lost knight hears his comrades sing,
    And, near at hand, their bridles ring,

So welcome I these sounds and voices,
    These airs from far-off summer blown,
    This life that leaves me not alone.

For the white glory overawes me;
    The crystal terror of the seer
    Of Chebar's vision blinds me here.

Rebuke me not, O sapphire heaven!
    Thou stainless earth, lay not on me
    This keen reproach of purity!

Let the strange frost-work sink and crumble,
    And let the loosened tree-boughs swing,
    Till all their bells of silver ring.

Shine warmly down, thou sun of noontime,
    On this chill pageant, melt and move
    The winter's frozen heart with love

And, soft and low, thou wind south-blowing,
    Breathe through a veil of tenderest haze
    Thy prophecy of summer days.

Come with thy green relief of promise,
    And to this dead, cold splendor bring
    The living jewels of the spring!

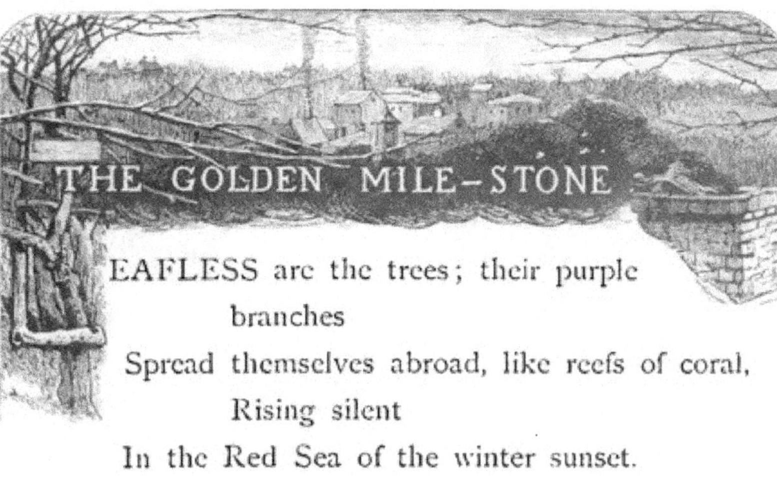

THE GOLDEN MILE-STONE

LEAFLESS are the trees; their purple
branches
Spread themselves abroad, like reefs of coral,
Rising silent
In the Red Sea of the winter sunset.

From the hundred chimneys of the village,
Like the Afreet in the Arabian story,
Smoky columns
Tower aloft into the air of amber.

At the window winks the flickering firelight;
Here and there the lamps of evening glimmer,
Social watch-fires
Answering one another through the darkness.

On the hearth the lighted logs are glowing,
And like Ariel in the cloven pine-tree
For its freedom
Groans and sighs the air imprisoned in them.

By the fireside there are old men seated,
Seeing ruined cities in the ashes,
Asking sadly
Of the Past what it can ne'er restore them.

By the fireside there are youthful dreamers,
Building castles fair, with stately stairways,
Asking blindly
Of the Future what it cannot give them.

By the fireside tragedies are acted
In whose scenes appear two actors only,
Wife and husband,
And above them God the sole spectator.

By the fireside there are peace and comfort,
Wives and children, with fair, thoughtful faces,
Waiting, watching,
For a well-known footstep in the passage.

Each man's chimney is his Golden Mile-stone;
Is the central point, from which he measures
Every distance
Through the gateways of the world around him.

In his farthest wanderings still he sees it;
Hears the talking flame, the answering night-wind,
As he heard them
When he sat with those who were, but are not.

Happy he whom neither wealth nor fashion,
Nor the march of the encroaching city,
Drives an exile
From the hearth of his ancestral homestead.

We may build more splendid habitations,
Fill our rooms with paintings and with sculptures,
But we cannot
Buy with gold the old associations!

A WINTER PIECE.

THE time has been that these wild solitudes,
Yet beautiful as wild, were trod by me
Oftener than now; and when the ills of life
Had chafed my spirit — when the unsteady pulse
Beat with strange flutterings — I would wander forth
And seek the woods. The sunshine on my path
Was to me as a friend. The swelling hills,
The quiet dells retiring far between,
With gentle invitation to explore
Their windings, were a calm society
That talked with me and soothed me. Then the chant
Of birds, and chime of brooks, and soft caress
Of the fresh sylvan air, made me forget
The thoughts that broke my peace, and I began
To gather simples by the fountain's brink,
And lose myself in day-dreams. While I stood
In Nature's loneliness, I was with one
With whom I early grew familiar, one

Who never had a frown for me, whose voice
Never rebuked me for the hours I stole
From cares I loved not, but of which the World
Deems highest, to converse with her. When shrieked

The bleak November winds, and smote the woods,
And the brown fields were herbless, and the shades
That met above the merry rivulet
Were spoiled, I sought, I loved them still; they seemed
Like old companions in adversity.
Still there was beauty in my walks; the brook,
Bordered with sparkling frost-work, was as gay

As with its fringe of summer flowers. Afar,
The village with its spires, the path of streams
And dim receding valleys, hid before
By interposing trees, lay visible
Through the bare grove, and my familiar haunts
Seemed new to me. Nor was I slow to come
Among them, when the clouds from their still skirts
Had shaken down on earth the feathery snow,
And all was white. The pure keen air abroad,
Albeit it breathed no scent of herb, nor heard
Love-call of bird nor merry hum of bee,
Was not the air of death. Bright mosses crept
Over the spotted trunks, and the close buds,
That lay along the boughs, instinct with life,
Patient, and waiting the soft breath of Spring,
Feared not the piercing spirit of the North.
The snow-bird twittered on the beechen bough,

And 'neath the hemlock, whose thick branches bent
Beneath its bright cold burden, and kept dry
A circle, on the earth, of withered leaves,
The partridge found a shelter. Through the snow
The rabbit sprang away. The lighter track
Of fox, and the raccoon's broad path, were there,
Crossing each other. From his hollow tree
The squirrel was abroad, gathering the nuts
Just fallen, that asked the winter cold and sway
Of winter blast to shake them from their hold.

But winter has yet brighter scenes, — he boasts
Splendors beyond what gorgeous Summer knows;
Or Autumn with his many fruits, and woods
All flushed with many hues. Come when the rains
Have glazed the snow, and clothed the trees with ice,
While the slant sun of February pours
Into the bowers a flood of light. Approach!
The incrusted surface shall upbear thy steps,
And the broad arching portals of the grove
Welcome thy entering. Look! the massy trunks

Are cased in the pure crystal; each light spray,
Nodding and tinkling in the breath of heaven,
Is studded with its trembling water-drops,
That glimmer with an amethystine light.
But round the parent stem the long low boughs
Bend, in a glittering ring, and arbors hide

The glassy floor. Oh! you might deem the spot
The spacious cavern of some virgin mine,
Deep in the womb of earth, — where the gems grow,
And diamonds put forth radiant rods and bud
With amethyst and topaz, — and the place
Lit up, most royally, with the pure beam
That dwells in them. Or haply the vast hall
Of fairy palace, that outlasts the night,
And fades not in the glory of the sun; —
Where crystal columns send forth slender shafts
And crossing arches; and fantastic aisles
Wind from the sight in brightness, and are lost
Among the crowded pillars. Raise thine eye;
Thou seest no cavern roof, no palace vault;
There the blue sky and the white drifting cloud
Look in. Again the wildered fancy dreams
Of spouting fountains, frozen as they rose,
And fixed, with all their branching jets, in air,
And all their sluices sealed. All, all is light;
Light without shade. But all shall pass away
With the next sun. From numberless vast trunks
Loosened, the crashing ice shall make a sound
Like the far roar of rivers, and the eve
Shall close o'er the brown woods as it was wont.

And it is pleasant, when the noisy streams
Are just set free, and milder suns melt off

The plashy snow, save only the firm drift
In the deep glen or the close shade of pines, —
'T is pleasant to behold the wreaths of smoke
Roll up among the maples of the hill,
Where the shrill sound of youthful voices wakes
The shriller echo, as the clear pure lymph,
That from the wounded trees, in twinkling drops

Falls, mid the golden brightness of the morn,
Is gathered in with brimming pails, and oft,
Wielded by sturdy hands, the stroke of axe
Makes the woods ring. Along the quiet air
Come and float calmly off the soft light clouds,
Such as you see in summer, and the winds
Scarce stir the branches. Lodged in sunny cleft,
Where the cold breezes come not, blooms alone
The little wind-flower, whose just opened eye
Is blue as the spring heaven it gazes at,
Startling the loiterer in the naked groves
With unexpected beauty, for the time
Of blossoms and green leaves is yet afar.
And ere it comes, the encountering winds shall oft
Muster their wrath again, and rapid clouds
Shade heaven, and bounding on the frozen earth
Shall fall their volleyed stores, rounded like hail
And white like snow, and the loud North again
Shall buffet the vexed forest in his rage.

THE FIRST SNOW-FALL.

THE snow had begun in the gloaming,
  And busily all the night
Had been heaping field and highway
  With a silence deep and white.

Every pine and fir and hemlock
  Wore ermine too dear for an earl,
And the poorest twig on the elm-tree
  Was ridged inch deep with pearl.

From sheds new-roofed with Carrara
  Came Chanticleer's muffled crow,
The stiff rails were softened to swan's-down,
  And still fluttered down the snow.

I stood and watched by the window
  The noiseless work of the sky,
And the sudden flurries of snow-birds,
  Like brown leaves whirling by.

I thought of a mound in sweet Auburn
  Where a little headstone stood;
How the flakes were folding it gently,
  As did robins the babes in the wood.

Up spoke our own little Mabel,
  Saying, "Father, who makes it snow?"
And I told of the good All-Father
  Who cares for us here below.

Again I looked at the snow-fall,
  And thought of the leaden sky
That arched o'er our first great sorrow,
  When that mound was heaped so high.

I remembered the gradual patience
  That fell from that cloud like snow,
Flake by flake, healing and hiding
  The scar of our deep-plunged woe.

And again to the child I whispered,
  "The snow that husheth all,
Darling, the merciful Father
  Alone can make it fall!"

Then, with eyes that saw not, I kissed her;
And she, kissing back, could not know
That *my* kiss was given to her sister,
Folded close under deepening snow.

IN SCHOOL-DAYS.

STILL sits the school-house by the road,
A ragged beggar sunning;
Around it still the sumachs grow,
And blackberry-vines are running.

Within, the master's desk is seen,
Deep scarred by raps official;
The warping floor, the battered seats,
The jack-knife's carved initial;

The charcoal frescos on its wall;
Its door's worn sill, betraying
The feet that, creeping slow to school,
Went storming out to playing!

It touched the tangled golden curls,
  And brown eyes full of grieving,
Of one who still her steps delayed
  When all the school were leaving.

For near her stood the little boy
  Her childish favor singled;
His cap pulled low upon a face
  Where pride and shame were mingled.

Pushing with restless feet the snow;
  To right and left, he lingered; —
As restlessly her tiny hands
  The blue-checked apron fingered.

He saw her lift her eyes; he felt
  The soft hand's light caressing,
And heard the tremble of her voice,
  As if a fault confessing.

"I'm sorry that I spelt the word:
  I hate to go above you,
Because," — the brown eyes lower fell, —
  "Because, you see, I love you!"

Long years ago a winter sun
  Shone over it at setting;
Lit up its western window-panes,
  And low eaves' icy fretting.

Still memory to a gray-haired man
  That sweet child-face is showing,
Dear girl! the grasses on her grave
  Have forty years been growing!

He lives to learn, in life's hard school,
  How few who pass above him
Lament their triumph and his loss,
  Like her, — because they love him.

THE SNOW-SHOWER.

STAND here by my side and turn, I pray,
  On the lake below thy gentle eyes;
The clouds hang over it, heavy and gray,
  And dark and silent the water lies;
And out of that frozen mist the snow
In wavering flakes begins to flow;
                    Flake after flake
They sink in the dark and silent lake.

See how in a living swarm they come
  From the chambers beyond that misty veil;
Some hover awhile in air, and some
  Rush prone from the sky like summer hail.
All, dropping swiftly or settling slow,
Meet, and are still in the depths below;
          Flake after flake
Dissolved in the dark and silent lake.

Here delicate snow-stars, out of the cloud,
  Come floating downward in airy play,
Like spangles dropped from the glistening crowd
  That whiten by night the milky-way;
There broader and burlier masses fall;
The sullen water buries them all —
          Flake after flake —
All drowned in the dark and silent lake.

And some, as on tender wings they glide
  From their chilly birth-cloud, dim and gray,
Are joined in their fall, and, side by side,
  Come clinging along their unsteady way;
As friend with friend, or husband with wife
Makes hand in hand the passage of life;
          Each mated flake
Soon sinks in the dark and silent lake.

Lo! while we are gazing, in swifter haste
  Stream down the snows, till the air is white,
As, myriads by myriads madly chased,
  They fling themselves from their shadowy height,
The fair, frail creatures of middle sky,
What speed they make, with their grave so nigh;
                Flake after flake,
To lie in the dark and silent lake!

I see in thy gentle eyes a tear.;
  They turn to me in sorrowful thought:
Thou thinkest of friends, the good and dear,
  Who were for a time, and now are not;
Like these fair children of cloud and frost,
That glisten a moment and then are lost,
            Flake after flake,—
All lost in the dark and silent lake.

Yet look again, for the clouds divide;
  A gleam of blue on the water lies;
And far away, on the mountain-side,
  A sunbeam falls from the opening skies.
But the hurrying host that flew between
The cloud and the water no more is seen;
            Flake after flake,
At rest in the dark and silent lake.

WOODS IN WINTER.

WHEN winter winds are piercing chill,
  And through the hawthorne blows the gale,
With solemn feet I tread the hill,
  That overbrows the lonely vale.

O'er the bare upland, and away
  Through the long reach of desert woods,
The embracing sunbeams chastely play,
  And gladden these deep solitudes.

Where, twisted round the barren oak,
The summer vine in beauty clung,
And summer winds the stillness broke,
The crystal icicle is hung.

Where, from their frozen urns, mute springs
Pour out the river's gradual tide,
Shrilly the skater's iron rings,
And voices fill the woodland side.

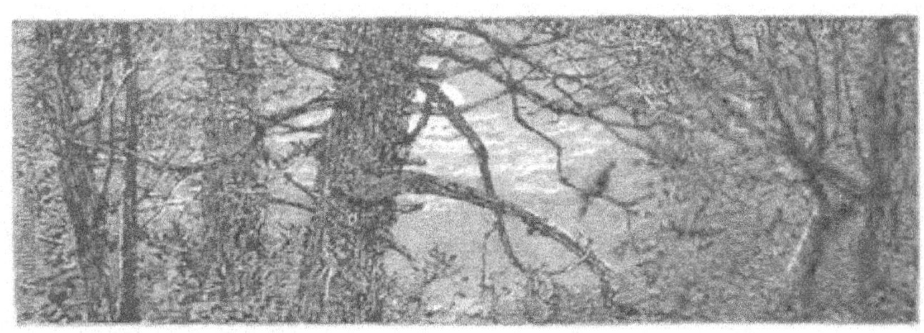

Alas! how changed from the fair scene,
When birds sang out their mellow lay,
And winds were soft, and woods were green,
And the song ceased not with the day!

But still wild music is abroad,
  Pale, desert woods! within your crowd;
And gathering winds, in hoarse accord,
  Amid the vocal reeds pipe loud.

Chill airs and wintry winds! my ear
  Has grown familiar with your song;
I hear it in the opening year,—
  I listen, and it cheers me long.

THE SNOW-STORM.

ANNOUNCED by all the trumpets of the sky,
Arrives the snow, and, driving o'er the fields,
Seems nowhere to alight: the whited air
Hides hills and woods, the river, and the heaven,
And veils the farm-house at the garden's end.
The sled and traveller stopped, the courier's feet
Delayed, all friends shut out, the housemates sit
Around the radiant fireplace, enclosed
In a tumultuous privacy of storm.

Come see the north-wind's masonry
Out of an unseen quarry evermore
Furnished with tile, the fierce artificer
Curves his white bastions with projected roof
Round every windward stake, or tree, or door
Speeding, the myriad-handed, his wild work
So fanciful, so savage, naught cares he

For number or proportion.
Mockingly,
On coop or kennel he hangs
Parian wreaths;
A swan-like form invests the hidden
thorn;

Fills up the farmer's lane from wall to wall,
Maugre the farmer's sighs; and, at the gate,
A tapering turret overtops the work.
And when his hours are numbered, and the world
Is all his own, retiring, as he were not,
Leaves, when the sun appears, astonished Art
To mimic in slow structures, stone by stone,
Built in an age, the mad wind's night-work,
The frolic architecture of the snow.

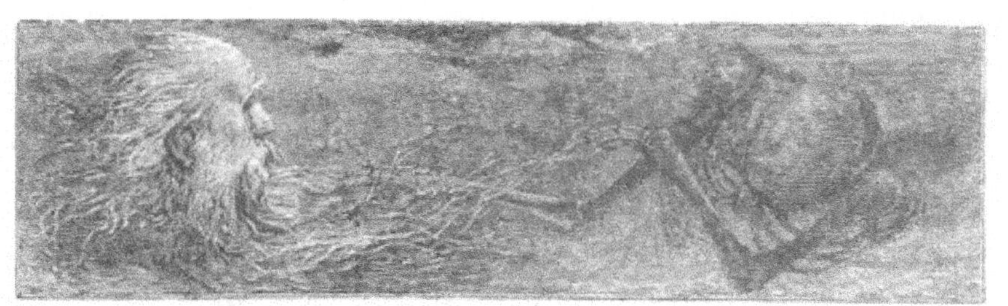

MIDNIGHT MASS FOR THE DYING YEAR.

YES, the Year is growing old,
  And his eye is pale and bleared!
Death, with frosty hand and cold,
  Plucks the old man by the beard,
    Sorely, sorely!

The leaves are falling, falling,
  Solemnly and slow;
Caw! caw! the rooks are calling,
  It is a sound of woe,
    A sound of woe!

Through woods and mountain passes
  The winds, like anthems, roll;
They are chanting solemn masses,
  Singing, "Pray for this poor soul,
    Pray, pray!"

And the hooded clouds, like friars,
  Tell their beads in drops of rain,
And patter their doleful prayers;
  But their prayers are all in vain,
    All in vain!

There he stands in the foul weather,
  The foolish, fond Old Year,
Crowned with wild-flowers and with heather,
  Like weak, despised Lear,
    A king, a king!

Then comes the summer-like day,
  Bids the old man rejoice!
His joy! his last! O, the old man gray,
  Loveth that ever-soft voice,
    Gentle and low.

To the crimson woods he saith,
  To the voice gentle and low
Of the soft air, like a daughter's breath,
  "Pray do not mock me so!
    Do not laugh at me!"

And now the sweet day is dead:
  Cold in his arms it lies:
No stain from its breath is spread
  Over the glassy skies,
    No mist or stain!

Then, too, the Old Year dieth,
  And the forests utter a moan,
Like the voice of one who crieth
  In the wilderness alone,
    "Vex not his ghost!"

Then comes, with an awful roar,
Gathering and sounding on,
The storm-wind from Labrador,
The wind Euroclydon,
The storm-wind!

Howl! howl! and from the forest
Sweep the red leaves away!
Would the sins that thou abhorrest,
O Soul! could thus decay,
And be swept away!

For there shall come a mightier blast,
There shall be a darker day:
And the stars, from heaven down-cast,
Like red leaves be swept away!
Kyrie eleyson!
Christe, eleyson!

CAMBRIDGE, MASS

www.ingramcontent.com/pod-product-compliance
Lightning Source LLC
Chambersburg PA
CBHW022037080426
42733CB00007B/868

* 9 7 8 3 3 3 7 2 5 6 9 1 3 *